365 DAYS OF

Buddha
Wisdom

QUOTES FROM BUDDHIST THINKERS
TO BRING YOU DAILY INSPIRATION

summersdale

An Hachette UK Company
www.hachette.co.uk

Summersdale Publishers
Part of Octopus Publishing Group Limited
Carmelite House
50 Victoria Embankment
LONDON
EC4Y 0DZ
UK

www.summersdale.com

Printed and bound in Malaysia

ISBN: 978-1-83799-389-5

This FSC® label means
that materials used for
the product have been
responsibly sourced

MIX
Paper | Supporting
responsible forestry
FSC® C016973

Substantial discounts on bulk quantities of Summersdale books are available to corporations, professional associations and other organizations. For details contact general enquiries: telephone: +44 (0) 1243 771107 or email: enquiries@summersdale.com.

To ....

From ....

introduction

It's no secret that mindfulness is an essential part of Buddhism; in fact, it is considered the key to obtaining inner peace. Buddhism has inspired people across the globe to follow their own unique path towards mindful awakening. So, taking time out to achieve mindfulness amid the busyness of everyday modern life is a positive step towards a more peaceful existence.

This is the main message at the heart of this book. Each page offers a refreshing daily dose of wisdom from Buddhist teachers, scriptures, thinkers, those inspired by Buddhism, and the Buddha himself, who found profound awakening more than two and a half thousand years ago.

In having one piece of wisdom each day to contemplate and reflect on, you will be encouraged to live fully in the moment. This book is your gentle reminder to stay mindful, loving and compassionate, which, in turn, will enrich your daily life with a sense of purpose and connection.

With 365 quotes to digest, you can randomly turn the page and stop at a quote or search for one that relates to how you're feeling in that moment, or you can turn to today's date and receive a piece of daily wisdom. The choice is yours.

Brighten your world and let this book be a guide to the realization of your own truth and spiritual enlightenment.

january

Let go of the past, let go of the future,
let go of the present, and cross over
to the farthest shore of existence.

THE DHAMMAPADA, VERSE 348

**Good friends, companions, and associates
are the whole of the spiritual life.**

BUDDHA

• • • •

Compassion is the spontaneous wisdom of the heart. It's always with us. It always has been, and always will be.

YONGEY MINGYUR RINPOCHE

• • • 04 • • •

You need to love yourself. Love yourself so much to the point that your energy and aura rejects anyone who doesn't know your worth.

BILLY CHAPATA

● ● ● (05) ● ● ●

We are all here for some special reason.
Stop being a prisoner of your past.
Become the architect of your future.

ROBIN SHARMA

● ● ● (06) ● ● ●

**Meditation brings wisdom; lack of
meditation leaves ignorance. Know
well what leads you forward and
what holds you back, and choose
the path that leads to wisdom.**

BUDDHA

● ● ● (07) ● ● ●

Anytime is a good time to find a spot to
relax and be kind and open to all beings.

DZOGCHEN PONLOP RINPOCHE

08

We should always keep in mind
that nothing is permanent. Only
then can we see the changes in our
daily lives are not that bad, so long
as we can face and adapt to them.

POMNYUN

• • • 09 • • •

The root of suffering is attachment.

BUDDHA

If you want to be loved, love others first.

LAMA ZOPA RINPOCHE

A great human revolution in just a single individual... will enable a change in the destiny of all humankind.

DAISAKU IKEDA

•••(12)•••

Hatred is never appeased by hatred in this world. By non-hatred alone is hatred appeased. This is a law eternal.

BUDDHA

13

One should train in deeds of merit – generosity,
a balanced life, developing a loving mind
– that yield long-lasting happiness.

BUDDHA

14

**Our life is in our hands. We are the
ones who help create our fate.**

MICHELLE YEOH

••• •••

It is my conviction that there is no way to peace – peace is the way.

THÍCH NHẤT HẠNH

••• (16) •••

The philosophy I've embraced isn't about sitting under a tree and studying my navel. It's about studying what's going on in my life and using the fuel to go on and live a bigger life.

ORLANDO BLOOM

Should someone do good, let them do it again
and again. They should develop this habit, for
the accumulation of goodness brings joy.

BUDDHA

●●● 18 ●●●

**The only thing stronger than fear is
knowing the truth of our connectedness.**

TARA BRACH

The greatest wisdom is seeing through appearances.

ATIŚA

••• 20 •••

A hero is one who heals their own wounds and then shows others how to do the same.

YUNG PUEBLO

21

Practice is not about getting: it's about letting go.

DAE KWANG

22

The Enlightened One is deep, boundless, hard to fathom, like the ocean.

BUDDHA

23

A closed window or door will cut one
off from the outside; a closed mind
will confine the space of thoughts.

HSING YUN

●●● **24** ●●●

**If everyone does some good, think
of what a good world this will be.**

JACKIE CHAN

●●● **25** ●●●

If we are forever blaming our difficulties on
others, this is a sure sign that there are still many
problems and faults within our own mind.

KELSANG GYATSO

No art or learning is to be pursued halfheartedly.

MURASAKI SHIKIBU

All you have to do is decide that wherever you are is the best place there is.

SODŌYOKOYAMA

●●● ●●●

**Let none find fault with others;
let none see the omissions and
commissions of others. But let one
see one's own acts, done and undone.**

BUDDHA

●●● (29) ●●●

Life is a circle of happiness, sadness, hard times
and good times. If you are going through hard
times, have faith that good times are on the way.

ANONYMOUS

Beyond the gift of material things, another dimension of generosity can also be the gift of time and attention, especially when others are suffering in bodily or mental pain.

BHIKKHU ANĀLAYO

The moment we decide things don't have to be a certain way, we create the possibility that they could be better than we know to imagine them.

LORI DESCHENE

february

It's a good thing to be satisfied with what one has.

BUDDHA

Awareness is the quintessential teaching of the Buddha – from the awareness of cool air as you breathe in and then out, to the profound awareness of natural perfection.

KHYENTSE NORBU

**Searching for happiness leads
to more searching. We'll find
it when we stop looking.**

GELONG THUBTEN

Like the Lotus flower that grows out of muddy
water but stays untouched by the mud, engage
in life without cherishing envy or hatred; live
in the world not a life of self but of truth.

AŚVAGHOSA

**I have always believed, and
I still believe, that whatever
good or bad fortune may come
our way we can always give
it meaning and transform it
into something of value.**

HERMANN HESSE

A noble one produces an abundance
of merit by having a compassionate
mind towards all living beings.

BUDDHA

••• 07 •••

You can measure the depth of a person's
awakening by how they serve others.

KŪKAI

••• 08 •••

**Having a positive experience and
not appreciating it is like having
a gift and not unwrapping it.**

BODHIPAKSA

••• 09 •••

No anger inside means no enemy outside.

LAMA ZOPA RINPOCHE

A wise person should be urgently moved on occasions that make for urgency.

BUDDHA

There is no other difficult practice equal
to patience – not getting angry with
someone who harms you, and even if
you do get angry, not remaining so.

KANGYUR RINPOCHE

In the midst of movement and chaos,
keep stillness inside of you.

DEEPAK CHOPRA

**Loving-kindness is the thought of
wishing total happiness for others
and putting that wish into practice.**

TULKU THONDUP

Most of the things I've come away with from Buddhism have been human – understanding feelings, impermanence, and trying to understand other people and where they're coming from.

KEANU REEVES

••• (15) •••

By relying upon me as a good friend – beings are freed from sorrow, lamentation, pain, displeasure, and despair.

BUDDHA

••• 16 •••

We can all bring about change. We can bring
about greater equality for all, and that,
I feel, is part of the mission of Buddhism.

GEORGE TAKEI

••• 17 •••

**Remember, if you are not speaking it,
you are storing it, and that gets heavy.**

ANONYMOUS

••• 18 •••

We all miss out when we close our minds and
borders to global understanding of one another.

SHARON STONE

The most fundamental aggression to ourselves, the most fundamental harm we can do to ourselves, is to remain ignorant by not having the courage and the respect to look at ourselves honestly and gently.

PEMA CHÖDRÖN

••• 20 •••

Just as a mother would protect her only child with her life, even so let one cultivate a boundless love towards all beings.

BUDDHA

The difference between misery and happiness
depends on what we do with our attention.

SHARON SALZBERG

**A kind gesture can reach a wound
that only compassion can heal.**

STEVE MARABOLI

**Three things shine before the world
and cannot be hidden. They are
the moon, the sun and the truth
proclaimed by the Tathāgata.**

LAKSHMI NARASU

• • • (24) • • •

The thing that is disliked by me is also
disliked by others. Since I dislike this thing,
how can I inflict it on someone else?

BUDDHA

••• 25 •••

No one saves us but ourselves. No one can and
no one may. We ourselves must walk the path.

PAUL CARUS

••• 26 •••

**Walk as if you are kissing the
Earth with your feet.**

THÍCH NHẤT HẠNH

••• 27 •••

You are an aperture through which the
universe is looking at and exploring itself.

ALAN WATTS

● ● ● (28) ● ● ●

A disciplined mind brings happiness.

BUDDHA

● ● ● (29) ● ● ●

With self-compassion, we give ourselves the same
kindness and support we'd give to a good friend.

KRISTIN NEFF

march

In this and every future lifetime, may I
be able to benefit all sentient beings.

KHENCHEN TSULTRIM LODRÖ

**The privilege of a lifetime
is being who you are.**

JOSEPH CAMPBELL

Conquer anger with non-anger.
Conquer badness with goodness.
Conquer meanness with generosity.
Conquer dishonesty with truth.

BUDDHA

If we learn to open our hearts, anyone, including
the people who drive us crazy, can be our teacher.

PEMA CHÖDRÖN

••• • 05 • •••

We all wish for world peace, but world
peace will never be achieved unless we first
establish peace within our own minds.

KELSANG GYATSO

••• • 06 • •••

**Activity and rest are two vital
aspects of life. To find a balance
in them is a skill in itself.**

SRI SRI RAVI SHANKAR

••• • 07 • •••

Running away from your problems
is a race you'll never win. You cannot
heal what you refuse to face.

ANONYMOUS

Treat every moment as your last. It is
not preparation for something else.

SHUNRYŪ SUZUKI

•••(09)•••

If your compassion does not include
yourself, it is incomplete.

JACK KORNFIELD

•••(10)•••

All experiences are preceded by mind,
having mind as their master, created by mind.

BUDDHA

••• •••

If you can recognize and accept your pain
without running away from it, you will
discover that although pain is there, joy
can also be there at the same time.

THÍCH NHẤT HẠNH

••• •••

Live being true to the single purpose of the moment.

YAMAMOTO TSUNETOMO

Meditation is simply getting to know your mind.

DZOGCHEN PONLOP RINPOCHE

Life is short. Be kind.

BODHIPAKSA

••• (15) •••

You are never more essentially, more
deeply, yourself than when you are still.

ECKHART TOLLE

Drop by drop is the water pot filled.
Likewise, the wise man, gathering it little
by little, fills himself with good.

BUDDHA

**Attention is the rarest and
purest form of generosity.**

SIMONE WEIL

If you let go a little you will have a little peace; if you let go a lot you will have a lot of peace; if you let go completely you will have complete peace.

AJAHN CHAH

Meditation and praying change your spirit into something positive. If it is already positive, it makes it better.

TINA TURNER

••• (20) •••

Meditation has been the most helpful and life-changing thing for me.

KATE HUDSON

••• (21) •••

Meditate... do not delay, lest you later regret it.

BUDDHA

Not thinking about anything is Zen.
Once you know this, walking, sitting,
or lying down, everything you do is Zen.

BODHIDHARMA

●●● (23) ●●●

**Without giving up hope – that there's
somewhere better to be, that there's
someone better to be – we will never
relax with where we are or who we are.**

PEMA CHÖDRÖN

●●● (24) ●●●

Without inner peace, outer peace is impossible.

KELSANG GYATSO

Education must inspire the faith
that each of us has both the
power and responsibility to effect
positive change on a global scale.

DAISAKU IKEDA

As I am, so are they; as they are, so am I.

BUDDHA

••• (27) •••

Freedom is not something you look for
outside of yourself. Freedom is within you.

AKONG RINPOCHE

••• (28) •••

**Peace is the art of etiquette; talking
softly is the mark of civilization;
smiling is the sunshine of relationships;
trust is the friend of success.**

HSING YUN

••• (29) •••

Patience gives you joy in the
process of awakening.

TARA BRACH

••• **30** •••

Sitting quietly, doing nothing, Spring
comes, and the grass grows, by itself.

MATSUO BASHŌ

••• **31** •••

**The brilliant light of your own awareness
shines everywhere, at all times.**

YONGEY MINGYUR RINPOCHE

april

If with a pure mind a person speaks
or acts, happiness follows them like
a never-departing shadow.

BUDDHA

**One of Buddhism's main practices
is understanding and experiencing
compassion, and how that ultimately
is a road to happiness.**

GOLDIE HAWN

•••● (03) ●•••

If you love yourself it doesn't matter if other
people don't like you because you don't need
their approval to feel good about yourself.

LORI DESCHENE

•••● (04) ●•••

**Your attention is like water, wherever you
put it, is what you're helping to grow.**

KAREN SALMANSOHN

•••● (05) ●•••

One who has spiritual friends abandons what is
unwholesome and develops what is wholesome.

BUDDHA

06

We long for permanence, but everything in the known universe is transient.

SHARON SALZBERG

07

Just know yourself, this is your witness.

AJAHN CHAH

Pain is important: how we evade it,
how we succumb to it, how we deal
with it, how we transcend it.

AUDRE LORDE

**Should a seeker not find a companion
who is better or equal, let them
resolutely pursue a solitary course.**

BUDDHA

You have to make peace with yourself. The
key is to find the harmony in what you have.

NAOMI WATTS

Not till your mind is motionless as wood or
stone, will you be on the right road to the Gate.

HUANGBO XIYUN

••• 12 •••

**Wherever you are, you are one
with the clouds and one with
the sun and the stars you see.**

SHUNRYU SUZUKI

••• 13 •••

Though the view should be as vast as the sky,
keep your conduct as fine as barley flour.

PADMASAMBHAVA

Be calm, kind and clear. This is the
most valuable thing we human beings
can learn, train in and master.

CHÖKYI NYIMA RINPOCHE

It is never too late to turn on the light.

SHARON SALZBERG

Simply let experience take place very freely,
so that your open heart is suffused with
the tenderness of true compassion.

TSOKNYI RINPOCHE

**The energy of happiness exists
in living today with roots sunk
firmly in reality's soil.**

DAISAKU IKEDA

●●●● 18 ●●●

A friend gives what is hard to give, and does
what's hard to do. They put up with harsh
words, and with things hard to endure.

BUDDHA

19

Every person is a world to explore.

THÍCH NHẤT HẠNH

20

**One of the greatest awakenings
comes when you realize that not
everybody changes. Some people
never change. And that's their journey.
It's not for you to fix them.**

ANONYMOUS

Let go of your judgement. Smile at your
hindrances. See them as quirky old
friends, rather than as mortal enemies.

BODHIPAKSA

••• (22) •••

**Searching outside of you is
Samsara (the world). Searching
within you leads to Nirvana.**

AMIT RAY

••• (23) •••

What may look like a small act of
courage is courage nevertheless.

DAISAKU IKEDA

24

When we are aware of our weaknesses
or negative tendencies, we open the
opportunity to work on them.

ALLAN LOKOS

25

**In whom there is no sympathy for living
beings: know him as an outcast.**

BUDDHA

26

You do not need to control the rain
if you can control your mind.

ALAN WATTS

The sun of real happiness shines in your
life when you start to cherish others.

LAMA ZOPA RINPOCHE

• • • (28) • • •

**When you repeatedly ignore your
intuition, you are betraying yourself.**

YUNG PUEBLO

●●● 29 ●●●

See them, floundering in their sense of mine,
like fish in the puddles of a dried-up stream
– and, seeing this, live with no mine, not
forming attachment for states of becoming.

BUDDHA

●●● 30 ●●●

**We have nothing to lose
by opening our hearts.**

DZOGCHEN PONLOP RINPOCHE

may

Every now and then it's good to stop climbing and
appreciate the view from right where you are.

LORI DESCHENE

This world belongs to all of us.

MICHELLE YEOH

••● (03) ●••

**Speak only endearing speech, speech
that is welcomed. Speech, when it brings
no evil to others, is a pleasant thing.**

BUDDHA

••● (04) ●••

Life contains within the end of life. When
we see that, we realize how precious life is.

BODHIPAKSA

If you want to succeed in the practice of
concentration, make it interesting.

THÍCH NHẤT HẠNH

•••(06)•••

**When life falls apart always remember
that this too will pass. Life will
have its unexpected turns.**

AJAHN BRAHM

•••(07)•••

We are many trees but one forest.

GELONG THUBTEN

08

If one wishes suffering not to
happen to the people and the
Earth, it begins with a kind heart.

PEMA CHÖDRÖN

••• **09** •••

**There is no fear for one whose
mind is not filled with desires.**

BUDDHA

••• (10) •••

It is my experience that the world itself
has a role to play in our liberation. Its very
pressures, pains, and risks can wake us
up — release us from the bonds of ego and
guide us home to our vast, true nature.

JOANNA MACY

••• (11) •••

**True compassion is undirected and
holds no conceptual focus. That kind
of genuine, true compassion is only
possible after realizing emptiness.**

TSOKNYI RINPOCHE

··· (12) ···

Gratitude is a gracious acknowledgement
of all that sustains us, a bow to our
blessings, great and small.

JACK KORNFIELD

··· (13) ···

**Love is when you think: How can I make
you happy? Attachment is when you think:
Why aren't you making me happy?**

DZOGCHEN PONLOP RINPOCHE

··· (14) ···

Whatever precious jewel there is in
the heavenly worlds, there is nothing
comparable to one who is Awakened.

BUDDHA

The coolness of Buddhism isn't indifference but
the distance one gains on emotions, the quiet
place from which to regard the turbulence.

REBECCA SOLNIT

**My religion is to live – and
die – without regret.**

MILAREPA

•••(17)•••

A peaceful life does not mean a life free of toil
and suffering, rather it means living without
being swayed no matter what happens. This
is a state of true peace and happiness.

DAISAKU IKEDA

• • • (18) • • •

The one in whom no longer exist the craving
and thirst that perpetuate becoming;
how could you track that Awakened one,
trackless, and of limitless range?

BUDDHA

• • • (19) • • •

**Happiness does not come from owning
lots of material wealth. True wealth is
in our heart. If our heart is not content,
we cannot be considered rich.**

CHENG YEN

20

Peace comes when our hearts are
open like the sky, vast as the ocean.

JACK KORNFIELD

21

Support the type of thinking that leads you to feeling good, peaceful and happy.

ALLAN LOKOS

22

Whatever has the nature of arising
has the nature of ceasing.

BUDDHA

23

If you want to take care of tomorrow, take better care of today.

DAININ KATAGIRI

For eternally and always there is only
now, one and the same now; the present
is the only thing that has no end.

ALAN WATTS

Our intention is to affirm this life, not to bring order out of chaos, nor to suggest improvements in creation, but simply to wake up to the very life we're living.

JOHN CAGE

●•● (26) ●•●

Strive always to be as kind, gentle and caring as possible towards all forms of sentient life.

AKONG RINPOCHE

••• (27) •••

To support mother and father, to cherish partner
and children, and to be engaged in peaceful
occupation – this is the greatest blessing.

BUDDHA

••• (28) •••

**May we continue to create the world
we believe in together, and may
the blessings of loving awareness
extend endlessly in all directions.**

TARA BRACH

••• (29) •••

There's a big difference between
having a thought and taking action.

SHARON SALZBERG

••• (30) •••

Understanding the true nature of things, or seeing things as they really are, is the ground of wisdom.

ALLAN LOKOS

••• (31) •••

Understanding is the heartwood
of well-spoken words.

BUDDHA

june

Whatever is not yours: let go of it.
Your letting go of it will be for your
long-term happiness and benefit.

BUDDHA

Everyone has the right to be happy no
matter what circumstance they are in.

POMNYUN

●●● (03) ●●●

**To see things as they are is to see the
potential of what they can become.**

BODHIPAKSA

●●● (04) ●●●

Sometimes we simply need to get out of our head
and give our heart some space to find the answer.

LORI DESCHENE

05

Always maintain a joyful mind. Appreciate the struggles as opportunities to wake up.

JEFF BRIDGES

06

Emulating consummate conviction... consummate virtue... consummate generosity... and consummate discernment. This is called admirable friendship.

BUDDHA

••• (07) •••

Practice is this life, and realization is this life,
and this life is revealed right here and now.

TAIZAN MAEZUMI

••• (08) •••

Nothing is impossible with confidence, perseverance, and courage.

CHENG YEN

••• (09) •••

Knowing life's purpose would invest
everything one did with meaning.

KENTETSU TAKAMORI

10

Our destination is never a place
but a new way of seeing things.

HENRY MILLER

11

**Our mind is like a cloudy sky:
in essence clear and pure, but
overcast by clouds of delusions.**

KELSANG GYATSO

If you find the mind wandering or you
find yourself struggling at a certain point,
just notice what's going on in the mind.

JON KABAT-ZINN

**Everyone makes mistakes. Whether we
put our mistakes to use depends on
how deeply we reflect on our actions.**

KENTETSU TAKAMORI

•••(14)•••

The only person you can change is
yourself. But when you change yourself,
then you change everything.

KAREN SALMANSOHN

••• (15) •••

Kindness is a basic sense of caring
that comes from the heart.

DZOGCHEN PONLOP RINPOCHE

••• (16) •••

**Just grasp the essence, don't
concern yourself with results.**

MUSŌ SOSEKI

••• (17) •••

Failure lies concealed in every success,
and success in every failure.

ECKHART TOLLE

••• (18) •••

Enduring patience is the highest austerity.

THE DHAMMAPADA, VERSE 184

••• (19) •••

I am a continuation like the rain
is a continuation of the cloud.

THÍCH NHẤT HẠNH

20

A mind unruffled by the
vagaries of fortune, from
sorrow freed, from defilements
cleansed, from fear liberated –
this is the greatest blessing.

BUDDHA

Happiness is a state of mind, therefore
the real source of happiness lies in the
mind, not in external circumstances.

KELSANG GYATSO

22

To practice Zen means to realize one's existence
in the beauty and clarity of this present moment.

PETER MATTHIESSEN

23

**Getting lost along your path is a part of
finding the path you are meant to be on.**

ROBIN SHARMA

24

If you follow self-cherishing thoughts,
those thoughts become your identity.

LAMA ZOPA RINPOCHE

••● (25) ●••

I believe there is an art to living...
Thankfully, even when I misstep, my Buddhist
practice keeps me on my right road.

ORLANDO BLOOM

••● (26) ●••

**With true compassion, we feel the
other person's experience as our
shared human vulnerability.**

TARA BRACH

Inner peace, less conflict.

GELONG THUBTEN

Know well what leads you forward
and what holds you back and choose
the path that leads to wisdom.

THE DHAMMAPADA, VERSE 282

••• (29) •••

To tame ourselves is the only way we
can change and improve the world.

AKONG RINPOCHE

••• (30) •••

As a water bead on a lotus leaf, as
water on a red lily, does not adhere,
so the sage does not adhere to the
seen, the heard, or the sensed.

BUDDHA

july

The only cause of happiness is love and
the only cause of suffering is ego.

GARCHEN RINPOCHE

**Life is only available in the present.
It is necessary to return to this moment
to be in touch with life as it really is.**

THÍCH NHẤT HẠNH

••• **03** •••

Just as a solid rock is not shaken by
the storm, even so the wise are not
affected by praise or blame.

BUDDHA

••• **04** •••

**The Buddha says that pain or
suffering arises through desire or
craving and that to be free of pain
we need to cut the bonds of desire.**

ECKHART TOLLE

••• **05** •••

Faith is the willingness to take the next step.

SHARON SALZBERG

Every second of this human life is more precious than skies of wish-granting jewels.

LAMA ZOPA RINPOCHE

Mindfulness is the awareness that emerges through paying attention, on purpose, in the present moment, and non-judgementally to the unfolding of experience moment by moment.

JON KABAT-ZINN

••• 08 •••

Let all-embracing thoughts for all beings be yours.

BUDDHA

••• 09 •••

In compassion, when we feel with the other,
we dethrone ourselves from the centre of our
world and we put another person there.

KAREN ARMSTRONG

••• 10 •••

**There is no more worldly existence for
the wise one who, like the earth, resents
nothing, who is firm as a high pillar and
as pure as a deep pool free from mud.**

THE DHAMMAPADA, VERSE 95

••• 11 •••

Simplicity is the whole secret of well-being.

PETER MATTHIESSEN

Give out what you most want to come back.

ROBIN SHARMA

True happiness means forging a strong
spirit that is undefeated, no matter
how trying our circumstances.

DAISAKU IKEDA

●●● (14) ●●●

Mind is like space because it has no limitation.
When there are no clouds, when it is completely
clear, space is like our "ordinary" state of mind.

LAMA YESHE RINPOCHE

●●● (15) ●●●

**Know from the rivers in clefts and in
crevices: those in small channels flow
noisily, the great flow silent. Whatever's not
full makes noise. Whatever is full is quiet.**

BUDDHA

●●● (16) ●●●

Love like someone's life depends on it.
Be compassionate, understanding, and kind.

LORI DESCHENE

Wisdom is always an overmatch for strength.

PHIL JACKSON

You are the sky. Everything else
– it's just the weather.

PEMA CHÖDRÖN

You can't stop the waves,
but you can learn to surf.

JON KABAT-ZINN

**You can't calm the storm, so stop
trying. What you can do is calm
yourself. The storm will pass.**

TIMBER HAWKEYE

● ● ● 21 ● ● ●

One is not called noble who harms living beings.
By not harming living beings one is called noble.

BUDDHA

••• (22) •••

We condemn in ourselves what
we find forgivable in others.

BODHIPAKSA

••• (23) •••

**Treat every living being, including
yourself, with kindness, and the world
will immediately be a better place.**

TIMBER HAWKEYE

••• (24) •••

Mindfulness and self-compassion both
allow us to live with less resistance
toward ourselves and our lives.

KRISTIN NEFF

••• (25) •••

**Should a person do good, let him
do it again and again. Let him
find pleasure therein, for blissful
is the accumulation of good.**

BUDDHA

••• (26) •••

Purity and impurity depend on oneself;
no one can purify another.

THE DHAMMAPADA, VERSE 165

Anger, fear, desire – all of these states can be a source of wisdom when they are acknowledged and felt with loving awareness.

JACK KORNFIELD

Freedom is not something you look for outside yourself. Freedom is within you.

AKONG RINPOCHE

••• 29 •••

The fullness of compassion manifests itself
as we feel and express care for ourselves
and for all who experience suffering.

TARA BRACH

••• 30 •••

**Do everything with a mind
that lets go. Don't accept praise
or gain or anything else.**

AJAHN CHAH

••• 31 •••

Let none find fault with others; let none
see the omissions and commissions of others.
But let one see one's own acts, done and undone.

BUDDHA

august

In the reservoir of life, time is limited.
Each morning as we open our eyes, we
should realize that there is only so much
time. Time unused is time wasted.

CHENG YEN

**You should train like this: "I will have good
friends, companions, and associates."**

BUDDHA

Kindness is fearless.

DZOGCHEN PONLOP RINPOCHE

**We will discover through our own
experience that this precious mind
of love is the real wish-granting jewel,
because it fulfills the pure wishes
of ourself and all living beings.**

KELSANG GYATSO

•••●(05)●•••

The purpose of our life is to help others through it.

PETER MATTHIESSEN

The path of truth leads us to
freedom and happiness.

POMNYUN

**Falling down and getting up explores
these timeless rhythms and the essential
skills needed to fully live our lives.**

MARK NEPO

•••(08)•••

As from a large heap of flowers many garlands
and wreaths can be made, so by a mortal in
this life there is much good work to be done.

THE DHAMMAPADA, VERSE 53

This kindness, in itself, is a means of awakening
the spark of love within you and helping others
to discover that spark within themselves.

TSOKNYI RINPOCHE

**Not by passing arbitrary judgements
does a man become just.**

THE DHAMMAPADA, VERSE 256

The wise do not grieve, having
realized the nature of the world.

BUDDHA

A loving, compassionate person heals others simply by existing.

THUBTEN ZOPA RINPOCHE

We will develop and cultivate the liberation of mind by loving-kindness, make it our vehicle, make it our basis, stabilize it, exercise ourselves in it, and fully perfect it.

BUDDHA

••• **14** •••

Those who have fifty dear ones have
fifty sufferings, those who have no
dear ones have no suffering.

BUDDHA

••• **15** •••

**Be kind to everyone without any cause;
be compassionate as we are all one.**

HSING YUN

••• **16** •••

Physical beauty that comes from keeping up
appearances can only be maintained temporarily,
but beauty that takes authenticity and sincerity
as its foundation is timeless and eternal.

CHENG YEN

••• (17) •••

Self-compassion is an antidote to self-pity.

KRISTIN NEFF

••• (18) •••

The calmed say that what is well-spoken is best; second, that one should say what is right, not unrighteous; third, what's pleasing, not displeasing; fourth, what is true, not false.

BUDDHA

••• (19) •••

The present moment is filled with joy and
happiness. If you are attentive, you will see it.

THÍCH NHẤT HẠNH

••• (20) •••

**Even death is not feared by
one who has lived wisely.**

JACK KORNFIELD

••• (21) •••

Every sentient being is equal to the Buddha.

TAI SITUPA

Over there are the roots of trees; over there, empty dwellings. Practice meditation, monks. Don't be heedless.

BUDDHA

● ● ● (23) ● ● ●

When the heart truly understands, it lets go of everything.

AJAHN CHAH

••• •••

Let go of all your fears.
Everything is always perfect.

PHẠM CÔNG THIỆN

••• •••

**One should therefore not rely on
mere words, but everywhere search
for the intention behind them.**

EDWARD CONZE

••• (26) •••

When watching after yourself,
you watch after others. When watching
after others, you watch after yourself.

BUDDHA

• • • (27) • • •

A smile is the most beautiful colour in the world.

HSING YUN

• • • (28) • • •

When life is going smoothly, we tend to lose ourselves in complacency. Small setbacks and challenges can actually awaken our conscience and help us grow.

CHENG YEN

• • • (29) • • •

Genuine happiness is found in courage.
Courage is the gateway to happiness.

DAISAKU IKEDA

• • • 30 • • •

It should be a pleasure and an honour to do our best and every moment is so wonderful and so precious – that is how our attitude should be.

TAI SITUPA

• • • 31 • • •

Mindfulness is when we observe our experience rather than merely participate in our experience.

BODHIPAKSA

september

May all beings have happy minds.

BUDDHA

**Identifying the pattern is awareness;
choosing not to repeat the cycle is growth.**

BILLY CHAPATA

••• (03) •••

Whatever we cultivate in times of ease,
we gather as strength for times of change.

JACK KORNFIELD

••• (04) •••

**True love should be transformative,
a process that amplifies our capacity to
cherish not just one person but all people.**

DAISAKU IKEDA

••• (05) •••

These two conditionings are universal: to long for
connection and to find ways to protect ourselves.

TARA BRACH

06

Smile, breathe, and go slowly.

THÍCH NHẤT HẠNH

●●● 07 ●●●

It takes no deep insight to see that the source
of both our well-being and our maladies
lies within our own hearts and minds.

B. ALAN WALLACE

●●● 08 ●●●

Irrigators channel waters; fletchers
straighten arrows; carpenters bend
wood; the wise master themselves.

BUDDHA

• • • (09) • • •

**Tomorrow and plans for tomorrow can
have no significance at all unless you are in
full contact with the reality of the present.**

ALAN WATTS

• • • (10) • • •

Whenever you deeply accept this moment
as it is – no matter what form it takes
– you are still, you are at peace.

ECKHART TOLLE

●●●(11)●●●

Your body is precious. It is your vehicle
for awakening. Treat it with care.

JACK KORNFIELD

●●●(12)●●●

**It is easy to see the faults of others,
but difficult to see one's own faults.**

THE DHAMMAPADA, VERSE 252

●●●(13)●●●

We are connected like one big family. Therefore,
love each other during peaceful times and
help each other when calamities strike.

CHENG YEN

That heartbeat of connection is discernible
when we learn to get a little quieter to hear it.

SHARON SALZBERG

**Use problems as ornaments, seeing them
as extremely precious, because they make
you achieve enlightenment quickly.**

LAMA ZOPA RINPOCHE

16

He who can curb his wrath as soon as
it arises, as a timely antidote will check
snake's venom that so quickly spreads, such
a monk gives up the here and the beyond,
just as a serpent sheds its worn-out skin.

BUDDHA

17

**We are not going in circles, we are
going upwards. The path is a spiral;
we have already climbed many steps.**

HERMANN HESSE

18

Compassion is truth in its purest form.

HSING YUN

The recognition of common humanity
entailed by self-compassion allows
us to be more understanding and less
judgemental of our inadequacies.

KRISTIN NEFF

**Meditation is a balancing act
between attention and relaxation.**

B. ALAN WALLACE

Every individual is an expression of
the whole realm of nature, a unique
action of the total universe.

ALAN WATTS

As the dawn is the forerunner of the sunrise, so spiritual friendships is the forerunner of the arising of the factors of enlightenment.

BUDDHA

Acknowledging the good that you already have in your life is the foundation for all abundance.

ECKHART TOLLE

You must recognize that your real enemy,
the thief that steals your happiness, is the
inner thief, the one inside your mind.

LAMA YESHE RINPOCHE

••• 25 •••

**When you are on your path, and it is truly
your path, doors will open for you where
there were no doors for someone else.**

JOSEPH CAMPBELL

••• 26 •••

The Buddhist principle is to be everybody's
friend, not to have any enemy.

AKONG RINPOCHE

The ones who cause suffering must also become the objects of your love.

THÍCH NHẤT HẠNH

They blame those who remain silent, they blame those who speak much, they blame those who speak in moderation. There is none in the world who is not blamed.

BUDDHA

29

Don't let your fear paralyze you. The scariest paths often lead to the most exciting places.

LORI DESCHENE

30

Just try to keep your mind in the present. Whatever arises in the mind, just watch it and let go of it.

AJAHN CHAH

october

Resolutely train yourself to attain peace.

BUDDHA

**Taking your seat in formal meditation
practice is actually taking a
significant stand in your life.**

JON KABAT-ZINN

Change is a transition between the way life was to the way life will be.

DZOGCHEN PONLOP RINPOCHE

Make deep connections, not deep attachments.

YUNG PUEBLO

• • • (05) • • •

Zen is a liberation from time. For if we open our eyes and see clearly, it becomes obvious that there is no other time than this instant.

ALAN WATTS

The two most powerful warriors are patience and time.

LEO TOLSTOY

Purity and impurity depend on oneself;
no one can purify another.

BUDDHA

Meditation means simple acceptance.

LAMA YESHE RINPOCHE

Happiness comes not from seeking pleasure and avoiding discomfort, but by meeting all of life's circumstances with mindfulness, compassion, and wisdom.

BODHIPAKSA

•••(10)•••

Sometimes letting things go is an act of far greater power than defending or hanging on.

ECKHART TOLLE

• • • (11) • • •

**Mindfulness allows you to live deeply
every moment that is given you to live.**

• • • (12) • • •

Good actions bring good results;
bad actions bring bad results.

AJAHN CHAH

13

Whenever we see something which
could be done to bring benefit to others,
no matter how small, we should do it.

AKONG RINPOCHE

14

**It is in the nature of things that joy
arises in a person free from remorse.**

BUDDHA

••• (15) •••

We're always trying to change the world
around us instead of recognizing that it's
our own attachment we have to change.

LAMA YESHE RINPOCHE

••• (16) •••

**It is precisely when we have suffered
defeat that we can determine to win
and open the path to future victory.**

DAISAKU IKEDA

Freedom and happiness are found in
the flexibility and ease with which
we move through change.

TAI SITUPA

**Those who cling to perceptions and views
wander the world offending people.**

BUDDHA

Maybe the fear is that we are less than
we think we are, when the actuality of
it is that we are much much more.

JON KABAT-ZINN

The emotion of compassion
springs from the recognition
that the human experience is
imperfect, that we are all fallible.

KRISTIN NEFF

The fact that I can plant a seed and it becomes a
flower, share a bit of knowledge and it becomes
another's, smile at someone and receive a smile
in return, are to me continual spiritual exercises.

LEO BUSCAGLIA

••• (22) •••

Putting onself in the place of another,
one should not kill nor cause another to kill.

BUDDHA

••• (23) •••

**Zen is the very awareness of the
dynamism of life living itself in
us – and aware of itself, in us, as
being the one life that lives in all.**

THOMAS MERTON

••• (24) •••

Peace can be made only by those
who are peaceful, and love can be
shown only by those who love.

ALAN WATTS

••• (25) •••

Try to eliminate the negative attitudes,
which bring suffering, and increase the
positive attitudes, which bring happiness.

LAMA ZOPA RINPOCHE

••• (26) •••

**Happiness comes when your work and
words are of benefit to yourself and others.**

JACK KORNFIELD

••• (27) •••

To flourish and keep evolving, we need to know
how to make peace with the truth of uncertainty.

TARA BRACH

••• (28) •••

**Realize deeply that the present
moment is all you have. Make the
Now the primary focus of your life.**

ECKHART TOLLE

••• (29) •••

Not to do any evil; to cultivate good;
to purify one's heart – this is the
teaching of all the Buddhas.

BUDDHA

••• (30) •••

**Sometimes sitting and doing nothing
is the best something you can do.**

KAREN SALMANSOHN

••• (31) •••

Gratitude isn't just about gratitude for the
good things... Gratitude can be for everything.

GELONG THUBTEN

november

Recognize these four good-hearted friends:
the helper, the friend in good times and bad,
the counsellor, and the one who's compassionate.

BUDDHA

**To be making steps on this
beautiful planet is a miracle.**

THÍCH NHẤT HẠNH

03

The past has no power over the present moment.

ECKHART TOLLE

04

The Buddha's enlightenment does not lie in "eradicating" earthly desires, but in infusing them with compassion and wisdom.

DAISAKU IKEDA

••• •••

Whatever obstacles arise, if you deal with
them through kindness without trying to
escape then you have real freedom.

AKONG RINPOCHE

••• •••

**Mindfulness practice means
that we commit fully in each
moment to be present.**

JON KABAT-ZINN

••• 07 •••

Better than a thousand useless words is one useful
word, upon hearing which one attains peace.

BUDDHA

••• •••

Only the impossible is worth doing.

AKONG RINPOCHE

••• (09) •••

The only way to bring peace to the earth is to learn to make your own life peaceful.

JACK KORNFIELD

••• (10) •••

The beginning of love is the will to let those we love be perfectly themselves.

THOMAS MERTON

**When we falter, we can forgive
ourselves and start again.**

SHARON SALZBERG

If your mind is happy, then you
are happy anywhere you go.

AJAHN CHAH

●●● (13) ●●●

There are no wrong turns, only unexpected paths.

MARK NEPO

●●● (14) ●●●

Just as the great ocean has one taste, the taste of salt, so also this teaching and discipline has one taste, the taste of liberation.

BUDDHA

●●● (15) ●●●

The minute you cherish others you have happiness and peace in your life.

LAMA ZOPA RINPOCHE

••• (16) •••

Wisdom springs from meditation;
without meditation wisdom wanes.

THE DHAMMAPADA, VERSE 282

••• (17) •••

**The smallest of actions is always better
than the noblest of intentions.**

ROBIN SHARMA

••• (18) •••

The best way to capture moments is to
pay attention. This is how we cultivate
mindfulness. Mindfulness means being awake.
It means knowing what you are doing.

JON KABAT-ZINN

Stay close to one so wise and astute who corrects you when you need it.

BUDDHA

There is no greater freedom than the
freedom to be what you are now.

ALAN WATTS

It takes only a flicker of the light of wisdom
to dispel the vast darkness of ignorance.

MILES NEALE

**We will develop and cultivate the
liberation of mind by loving kindness,
make it our basis, stabilize it, exercise
ourselves in it, and fully perfect it.**

BUDDHA

••• 23 •••

Sometimes, visualize that your heart is
a brilliant ball of light. As you breathe out,
it radiates rays of white light in all directions,
carrying your happiness to all beings.

DILGO KHYENTSE

24

Life can still be beautiful, meaningful,
fun, and fulfilling even if things don't
turn out the way you planned.

LORI DESCHENE

25

**When you recognize your problem comes
from your concept or your concept is
the problem, you don't blame others.**

LAMA ZOPA RINPOCHE

If a man going down into a river, swollen
and swiftly flowing, is carried away by the
current – how can he help others across?

BUDDHA

**Truth is not conceptual. We can
never understand or realize it
through concepts or ideas.**

ANAM THUBTEN RINPOCHE

•••(28)•••

Mindfulness should guide all your actions
and your spiritual endeavours.

DILGO KHYENTSE

• • • (29) • • •

I do not dispute with the world; rather it is the world that disputes with me.

BUDDHA

• • • (30) • • •

In the moments of remembering and trusting this basic goodness of our being, we open to happiness, peace, and freedom.

TARA BRACH

december

 01

A true friend is one who stands by you in need.

BUDDHA

 02

Slow down, get mindful, and try to enjoy the moment. This moment is your life.

LORI DESCHENE

03

If we can make just one other person
smile, at least there are two people smiling.
Then if both of you decide to bring a
smile to someone else, it will multiply.

DZOGCHEN PONLOP RINPOCHE

04

**In every one of us is a child who hopes
myths, mysteries, and dreams can
come true. They can, and they have.**

MILES NEALE

05

Delight in heedfulness! Guard well your thoughts!

BUDDHA

06

Ardently do today what must be done.

BUDDHA

We need to wake up and fall in love
with Earth. Our personal and collective
happiness and survival depends on it.

THÍCH NHẤT HẠNH

Patience is a form of wisdom. It demonstrates
that we understand and accept the fact that
sometimes things must unfold in their own time.

JON KABAT-ZINN

**True health shines in the lives of those
who continue to ardently devote
themselves to creating positive value
and the happiness of others.**

DAISAKU IKEDA

••• 10 •••

When you lose touch with inner stillness,
you lose touch with yourself.

ECKHART TOLLE

••• 11 •••

**Practice is not about getting; it is
about letting go. The more you let go,
the more you find yourself getting.**

DAE KWAN

••• 12 •••

Should you find a wise critic to point
out your faults, follow him as you
would a guide to hidden treasure.

BUDDHA

••• (13) •••

**For there is never anything but
the present, and if one cannot live
there, one cannot live anywhere.**

ALAN WATTS

••• (14) •••

Every living being has the potential to become a
Buddha, someone who has completely purified
his or her mind of all faults and limitations and
has brought all good qualities to perfection.

KELSANG GYATSO

Whoever doesn't flare up at someone
who's angry wins a battle hard to win.

BUDDHA

**For it's in facing the challenges of
daily life that we can really measure
our development of calmness,
insight, and compassion.**

YONGEY MINGYUR RINPOCHE

For a person of Zen, no limits exist. The blue
sky must feel ashamed to be so small.

MUSŌ SOSEKI

It is in doing that we learn. When we train,
sometimes it is easy, sometimes it is difficult,
but we keep coming back to the training.

AJAHN PASANNO

**Health is the greatest gift,
contentment is the greatest wealth.**

THE DHAMMAPADA, VERSE 204

● ● ● (20) ● ● ●

Less desire means less pain.

LAMA ZOPA RINPOCHE

··● (21) ●··

When we understand that we are not
separate from others, we begin to fathom
the preciousness of compassion.

GARCHEN RINPOCHE

··● (22) ●··

Hasten slowly and ye shall soon arrive.

JETSUN MILAREPA

··● (23) ●··

By meeting pain with a tender
presence, we transform our wounds
and losses into fierce grace.

TARA BRACH

Everyone wants happiness, but the
true way to reach perfect happiness
is to bring happiness to others.

DILGO KHYENTSE

•••(25)•••

**It's very important for us all to
understand that we are interconnected
and we need to hold hands together,
especially when the going gets tough.**

MICHELLE YEOH

•••(26)•••

Give, even if you only have a little.

BUDDHA

**Kindness begins with how
we treat our own thoughts.**

GELONG THUBTEN

Just this moment, just this breath, just this
sitting here, just this being human. Just this.

JON KABAT-ZINN

Radiate boundless love towards the entire world.

BUDDHA

**Take care of the present moment, and your
future experience will take care of itself.**

BODHIPAKSA

You yourself must strive.
The Buddhas only point the way.

BUDDHA

conclusion

As you reach the end of this journey, hopefully you feel more mindful, peaceful and fulfilled. It is well established that being respectful and showing loving-kindness and compassion to all living beings will make a positive difference in your own pursuit of happiness. With this in mind, you can continue to use the words of wisdom in this book to boost your gratitude, realize your potential and find inner peace. Understanding how to value yourself and others is all part of your own personal growth – a true awakening. As you continue your journey of self-discovery, allow these daily doses of mindfulness to guide you on your path to a more spiritual future.

also available

365 DAYS OF HEALING

ISBN: 978-1-83799-373-4

Quinn Clark

365 DAYS OF CALM

ISBN: 978-1-80007-443-9

Robyn Martin

365 DAYS OF INSPIRATION

ISBN: 978-1-80007-444-6

Robyn Martin

365 DAYS OF POSITIVITY

ISBN: 978-1-80007-102-5

Debbi Marco

365 DAYS OF KINDNESS

ISBN: 978-1-80007-100-1

Vicki Vrint

Have you enjoyed this book? If so, find us on Facebook at Summersdale Publishers, on Twitter/X at @Summersdale and on Instagram and TikTok at @summersdalebooks and get in touch. We'd love to hear from you!

www.summersdale.com

Image credits

Cover image © Rolau Elena/Shutterstock.com

Mandala icons throughout © venimo/Shutterstock.com